BARE & BREAKING

BARE & BREAKING

Karin Schimke

poems

Wie sê dat pyn terwyl dit woed

nie kan verwoord word nie –

tussen die primitiewe kreet

en die laaste burstende snik

tussen eina en amen

is daar baie klank-skakerings

– Sheila Cussons (from 'Ses op 'n tema', *Die Swart Kombuis*, 1978)

Who says that pain while it rages

cannot be worded –

between the primitive howl

and the last resigned sob

between ouch and amen

there are many sound-shades

– translated by Karin Schimke

PUBLICATION © MODJAJI BOOKS 2012

TEXT © KARIN SCHIMKE

FIRST PUBLISHED IN FEBRUARY 2012 BY MODJAJI BOOKS

PO BOX 385, ATHLONE, 7760, SOUTH AFRICA

http://modjaji.book.co.za

modjaji.books@gmail.com

ISBN 978-1-920397-97-5

EDITOR: GILL GIMBERG

BOOK AND COVER DESIGN: JACQUI STECHER

PRINTED AND BOUND BY MEGA DIGITAL, CAPE TOWN

SET IN GARAMOND

I

II

III

IV

I

Nameless Places

The narrow vertical trough between nose and lip
the skin inside an elbow or tucked behind a knee
the ellipses that snake around the tops of legs
where they join the torso
the valleys between toes
that link of ear to skull behind the lobes
the ridge of finger hold
between eyes –

a topographical lexicon
pauses in unwritten skin.

Let's begin.

Morning Work

We are cocked and angled
together like an African chair,
groin-hinged and eye-locked,
small-talking the sun up.
At the join we are genderless
until – out of two flat triangles –
something flowers at us,
blooms bright as though
our eyes are suns
and it must find light.
We give it light, and we laugh,
and then bury it, lids shut,
so it can seed again.

Ek Wil in Jou Mond Gaan Slaap

Ek wil in jou mond gaan slaap, opkrul
in die een of ander kies, jou tong
my kussing, jou tande
die paalheining wat glinster
wanneer die son deur mondhoeke ingly.

Ek wil insluimer waar ek sterredrome
teen jou verhemelte kan toets. Ek wil lê,
na aan jou larinks, neffens jou kleintong,
die gordyn waaragter jou gedagtes
woorde word, en wiegeliedjies maak.

For Two Voices

I.

In the broad dusk a winter Friday
she stood sideways to the mirror.
One foot and calf wrapped
in the mulberry leather of a heeled boot,
the other tip-toed naked for balance.
She pulled her dress up
to pull her knickers down
assessing whether –
without a gnawing panty-line –
her silhouette was smoother.
I saw her recently quivering thighs,
the dip of navel in the flat of stomach,
a swell, a puff, and then the dress
was down again.

I cannot say why this moved me so.

II.

In the solstice slant a late Tuesday's sun
he lay on his side, my leg cocked
over his hip. He spoke.
I don't know what he said.
His skin was creamy white;
mine was sallower, deeper. His
nipples were browner, and bigger;
mine, pinker and tighter. My arms
almost hairless, his chest sprouting
unevenly. But we both had freckles –
hot chocolate spattered star speckles –
and they ran all over his chest to spread
into the sky of my thigh as though
dispersed to a different universe.

I cannot say why this moved me so.

LANDING

I watched your face when as came last night
wave-rolling gently the years of freight
seabird caught in updraught flight
no labour   no breath   no weight
wingbones perforated newly light
looping an infinity eight
careening in on feather might
and landing beach placid not a second too late

Even So

I will scour
scrub and shear
season and dress
skin and debone
oil and salt
trim and truss.

I won't need to. You
love me already, would
have me raw.

Even so.

DOODLE YOU

I would like to borrow your body –
the entire athletic length and strength of it –
for one illegal weekend,
and doodle you.

On each sole, a mandala.
On each heel, blades of grass and dandelions.
On each foot, a scimitar
and on your right shoulder,
plump birds and faces and curlicues.
I will chart vines down your sides
and, around your navel, a loud flower.
Down your spine script words I love,
like "insouciance" and "belligerent",
like "emulate" and "obviate".
They will mean nothing,
but I could sound them for you.
I will lace and map your palms
and filigree and pattern your arms.
With my point three calligraphy pen, over your left nipple
I will draw a fat heart.

I want to doodle you.
I would like to borrow your body –
the entire athletic length and strength of it –
for one illegal weekend,
and doodle you.

THIS IS HOW WILLING

If grey speaks your eyes
and black curls your hair
if careful walks your feet
and sore swells your lips

If she (or she, or she) haunts you
and pity breaks you
and worry hobbles you
and weakness cracks you

If fear clatters your teeth
and nightmares dream you
if your tower crumbles
and you live only one more day

and never lift your hand again
to shield the darkness from your gaze
and only if your want reaches me
and only if your wounds let me

I will stand beside you
in the black cold cave
and let fireflies nest my hair.

Too Much

Everything was more:
limewash, neon
rock ballads, Wagnerian
sleep, toothy madness
dreams, softer
bodies, bolder
absence, the steep ascent towards plain exhilaration.

I am still sometimes stopped stock-still
by the blossoming crimson
roadkill
of what
love
was.

BREAKFAST

Your laughter breaks
over crusts and Special K and banana peels –
and always the small white circles of milk
spilt at the day's beginning.

THE GEOMETRY OF ORGASM

In this matter, the square on the hypotenuse is not equal

to its usual thing.

I mount the tubular trajectory wary or reluctant or breathless,
and wait for the skittering sands of geomancy to show the edge.

There is always an edge.
However gentle the rise.
There is always a fall.

Sometimes eighty degrees drops to a minor ledge.
Sometimes fifty gives way to a blossoming bungee.

I am the Pythagorean fire

or, sometimes, I am splayed
on the violence of an isosceles.

Jagged like shells or
broken like eggs. At times,
the surprising droop at the end of a line that meant to be straight
                                          but tired of infinity.

Always, the sublime isostasy
of tug and give,
slack and taut,

and the settling
triangulation of
going
coming
came.

BENDING

Bending to the will of your mouth
arching, plucking lilies from the air
the cool submission of me and you
the servile language of limbs
each moment tacking without
weariness to the next
the happy clank of the manacles
I carry back to you each time: here
I say, bind me again to your every jetty —

our journey is short.

All the Earth

Spring clouds are a new love's touch today
spooling flat hand across an immense sky,
gripping white-knuckled the distant mountain spine:
the pressure play of palm on skein,
and all the earth lonely for such careful fingering.

BLUE ROOM

When you took me in
your mouth
the blue room
got sucked in
and the rain
and the roses
the orchard
the mountains
the waterfall and
the tanned nap of the corn that circled wide.

The wide-circling corn, its nap tanned
our waterfall
these mountains
an orchard
heavy hung heads
of sweetest roses
the rain
this room
and I and my blues
were sucked into your mouth
when you took me in.

AS THE TIDE MOVES

I will turn my back to the moon.
I will turn my face to yours.
We will breathe each other's tide in the hot dark,
rise and fall together on this king-size raft
drifting through the suburban sea.
Shadows ripple across your face and shoulder.
Your limbs abandoned to the four corners
in chaotic rest. I will sleep neatly, and deep.
I have turned my back to the moon.

Shrinking

Once the world abounded around me and you:
our field for play was wide and little threatened.
The far borders arched us back from wandering
and we'd return with our mouths full of gifts.

Once we smiled at the small reunions of every day
and were relieved to breathe our otherness in each.
Now the space is smaller and we tread with thorny feet.
Our barbed voices tangle at every place –
even when we have nothing to say.

ONTMOETING

hier staan ons verbaas mekaar en aanstaar

    nog nie verlief
    nog nie vyandig
    die maat in oog geneem
    die einde in klip gebeitel

kom slyp jou tande teen myne
laat ons tweegeveg begin

SQUALL

You were so quiet I didn't see
the ocean turmoiling your greys.
You rocksteady stood by
watching the coming front,
and I softfell into the storm's eye.

GIVE US THIS DAY OUR DAILY CEASEFIRE

In the day we pass a package
between us: heavy with exasperation,
spiky with misunderstanding, alive with fury.

In sleep softened
we reach across it

across continents –

to palpate the flesh of "sorry"
and "I hate this"

never sure which to grasp:

these dumbly reaching limbs,
or that ticking package.

LENSMAN

You rolled in sand for me.
Frame by grainy frame,
you laughed carefully into my lens.

Your tits were perfect.

Later I butchered your post-coital
image into eight fragments –
pasted them on a piece of board
for some future husband to admire.

Your blameless gaze was a direct question

but in the end,
your perfume put me off.

BUTCHERED

Last night I let you carve me up:
axe for limbs, panga for head.
Last night you scalpelled out heartliverspleen
took a paring knife to fingers and toes
peeled my nails
skewered my tongue between two eyeballs.

Blue pupils leaked Colgate, choked on teeth.
In the name of the Mother, the Daughter, the Holy Psyche,
you anointed bloody parts with honesty.
We toasted your courage.

This morning I got up.
I stirred bits of skin into tea cups.
I put my ham on sandwiches,
mucous membranes for butter.

I walked.
I talked.
I worked.
Here is my choice.

GREEN WITH RAGE

Your rage is green.
Not like envy or inexperience.
Not like sapling bark,
or a cricket oval,
or a flutter of poplar leaves.

It is not the comforting arrogance of hospital-gown-green,
or casual green like your Diesel T-shirt.
Or gate-green,
or iceberg-lettuce-green.

Your rage rips at your khaki pupils:
it is a fast green
Peroni bottle
smashed
against
an alley wall
then thrust
under my chin.

And your rage is slow green:
old and petrified as freshest
lichen.

TIPPING POINT

Of course it was perfect: it could never outlast the night.

I remember tumbling
and tumbling all night
through hot sheets
and your mouth
and through sleep.

The day came late; it found us
drifting in the wreck.

COMMAS

Before we go into the day breaking
we make whole what we can:
my bare breasts
against your bare back,
your bare arse
in my bare lap –
We are the pauses in our own conversation
– let's break here.

There is nothing we cannot pause on
when we are bare and breaking.

SOS

In the night room, we read our loot,
speak in Braille, pronounce
joints and hinge bones – an eloquence
of sockets, lobes, fingertips.

I articulate ribs. You make a cup
of each hand for a scapula.
We tongue grooves, declaim
into the vaults of armpits,
whisper in the keyholes of navels.

We finger the stenography of spine,
translating tendons. Plosives
and vowels flutter around our
mute calamity. We are an emergency.
Urgent communiqués snap along
synapses. All is a tapping of Morse.

It's as though mouths,
as though lips, can
finish the words begun
by the o's and y's of our bodies.

CRASH

I don't know what I need.
I am disintegrating.

My friend phones and I push despair through underground
cables:
two thousand kilometres of grief stuffed into her good ear.

I don't know what I need.
I am disintegrating.

She phones my mother.
My mother comes.
She finds bits of me scattered across the floor.
Tears are shooting off the chandelier, snot
trails my dirty soles
through the unkempt house.
My mother holds me.
My legs go limp.
My mother's bent body holds me up.
My mother holds me up.

I don't know what I need.
I am disintegrating.

My mother phones my other friend.
He abandons his plans and *neuks* the N1 back home.
He grabs me by the scruff and pulls me up.
My friend's big body pulls me up.
My friend pulls me up.

I don't know what I need.
I am disintegrating.

My mother makes tea.
My friend gives me a pill.

Held and pulled and scraped,
all the pieces in pyjamas,
pink-pilled and pacified,
pillowed and pillared –

They know what I need.

III

THE WIND AT UILENSKRAALMOND

If the wind wears me down, peels me skin and pith
If the wind pops my fingers and knee caps
If it papers past membrane and wipes fluid
If the wind tears my hair and scatters it northsouth
If the wind pulls my nails and bends my neck
If it dries my eyes nose mouth
If the wind shakes heart liver
If it rattles skull
If it blows and cures
If it shears
If it scours me need-clean
If it sings my bones
If the wind wastes nothing wants nothing waits for nothing
If the wind browses the museum of my body
If it is the wind
It is this wind.

VERTIGO

she ran across the parquet slipped the flokati mat
crashed the window

no

she stood at the window prism looked up at sky bruise night
spread her

no

she tilted dived swanning spinning
tip-toed ink air
broke fingers first

no

she climbed the small gap the window gave
hung her finger joints clotted the view with frightened breath
fell ligament torn and sorry

no

she wandered to the glass hatch
watched tranquilised lights sputtering
leaned too hard fell faster than a bottle of Jack

    no

this is how it was:

drunk screaming she crashed the parquet with grief
roared the ungiving window frames which gave

she spangled spaghetti-like
ribbon-voiced
street lights crashed her

    no.

She did nothing.

HELLO DARLING

How lovely to see you.
How lovely to be lifted up,
legs and arms around you,
chest to chest, hug drunk.
How darling you are,
how we darling one another.
How darling we are.
How illicitly
and pointlessly
darling.

JY HET TWEE GESIGTE:

die een se oë is katsaggrys
die ander s'n is gruis

dansvoete flits
haak-en-steek
my nate los
tot als teen jou
verslap.

kalkklip en beton is jy,
tange jou hande
wat liefderik
papdruk.

álles in jou is twee

en ek haatlief jou
met my een
eenvoudige ekke.

CHOKING

You took each word from your mouth –
    glistening in the light of its own vowels,
    translated and buffed, each meaning
    morselled out, tongue and diphthong
    feeding sound and silence –
and placed it in the cup of my throat.

Now every remembered love word
sticks in my craw.

GEWELD

gee my 'n mes
laat ek jou uit my vlees kan kerf
laat ek jou soos murg uit my beendere kan skraap
en elke letter van jou heilige naam met 'n lem kan ontskryf.

VIOLENCE

give me a knife
to carve you from my flesh
to scrape you from my bones like marrow
and unwrite every letter of your holy name with a blade.

NEW BEGINNINGS TO OLD CONVERSATIONS

How shall we begin?

Shall we take each vial of vitriol
and toss it back and forth for a while.
Or would you prefer a thorough thrashing –
first of you, then of me.

Shall we begin at our beginning, or here, at our ending?

With small things (I am afraid, help me),
or big things (Sometimes I fucking despise you)?

Do we start at behaviour and work back to motivation,
conscious or unconscious, or do we begin at source
and pick our way towards the undoing in story form?

Shall we lay the blame mat first at your door
            for me to wipe my feet on,
or at my door for you to piss on as you pass through?

What is your proposal?

I'm looking for an original beginning, you see.

THE THING LOST

Something.
A key.
Something the length of a key.
Some shape.
Something the shape and length of a key.

The house wanders around itself
losing and finding
keys and goodbyes
the house finds ways to lose itself in
keys and byes   the walls stare
at paintings   numbly watching
mumbling the ways of losing things.
The house   without
lives   lost to it

finding something

but not the shape and length
of the keys that are lost.

BLIND ASSASSIN

A gun doesn't know its damage.
A bullet is senseless to its entry slide.
Skull shot trajects neither guilt nor empathy.

My stomach lies landmine still.
My prattle rattles soundless
AK attack attack.
I am the lovely insurgent
fingers flint and ignorant.
Gun powder sweats me:
I am your blue-eyed destroyer,
guerrilla bandit,
cacophonic trigger lover.

My thighs
my mouth
my eyes
conspire you,
plunder your bombshelter viscera,
snack blind, maggoting:
your death for my love.

I soldier on dumb as guns,
fingerprints all over your face.
Blood leaks down the barrel.
I pillage you innocent.
You make an arsenal of me.

Hair Salon

My hair is a swamp of creamy dye,
with highlights under neat foil folds.
My face in the mirror is a thickening
thing, and hard. I scratch my chest
with my mother's hand. The fine bones
on its back belie the thick squareness of
my *boere* palms. Its round nails have always
resisted femininity: these are hands for
making and mucking, for hefting and holding –
for drawing weary heads against this chest
I now scratch with a mother's aging hands.

The mirror's gaze is censure and approbation:
I am scarred shins and calloused shoulders.
The salon trance music plays against my body's struggle.
Stylists in heels and skirts murmur the importance of hair.

I stretch my neck to unfold the skin and remember:

I am here to grasp at something. Salvation and a root tint.
Relative importance is no longer a question. Each is the other.

KOEKERASIE

jou kop se hekelgoed
spin my hakke vloervas
jy struikel my
met jou omtoorwoorde
wikkel jy my toe
ek is ge-straightjacket
poespas geprobeer
gegom in jou web
disnis gemoker deur
jou sagvuisfascisme
vasgegordel in jou
paniekerige staanvlugte

dan knip jy hier 'n knoop
daar 'n hangtoutjie los
laat my val
'n duisend gekke stukkies
nege verdiepings moertoe
en al wat jy kan sê is:
jy verstaan my nie

maar jý het dit so gewil.

INDEPENDENCE DAY

The children slept right through the fourth of July.
You and I floated in their silence like awkward colleagues.

I can plot your moles.
I know your mother's secret.
I can tell you where you lost your Ray-Bans sixteen years ago
and which drawer holds your Patriarchal Blessing. I – only I –
have seen you cry. Now we skim nervous surfaces.

The children slept right through the fourth of July.

All the love we thought we had washed around our careful feet.
The ambivalent house surprised us with its nesty quiet.

We met at the fridge and smiled. I'll be honest:
I contemplated reversals on that weekend

the children slept right through the fourth of July.

IV

Unpacking Groceries

All the fruit feels wet today, all the apples,
the end-of-season clementines, bananas from the east coast:
they leave my fingers wet as I place them in the fruit bowl.

Outside last cold fronts silence the buds.
And the fruit is wet.
The fruit is wet as grief.

Die Vrede Gedig

Ek wou jou dood hê:

Kar		pille
Paal	of	val
Kis		as

iets doods
iets skadeloos

ek wou jou moor
my skedel oopbreek
en jou met bewevingers
glibberig uitvis
op 'n broodbord sit
en platdonner
met 'n vleisklopper
opsnipper met 'n naelskêrtjie
by die drein afspoel

maar jy's hard in my
jy vlie en keer terug
en ek is lam

lank kon ek soms jou kop borrelend
onder water hou met my linkerhand
terwyl die regterhand vir jou mooi
briewe skryf van al die lekker dinge,
dan pop jy skielik weer uit en ek:
"los los los my!" soos 'n dogtertjie
in 'n nagmerrie verstringel,
of soos daai bloody ou Macbeth vrou
met haar moordenaarsbloedkolletjie

maar ek kan jou nóg jou dig
nóg jou dans
nóg jou bestaan belet

kom vat my hand, ou kanniedood,
ek maak vir jou plek.
alleensaam met jou
moet ek leer lewe.

How Healed

How easy now the weight of you
I albatrossed my neck around
and lightfoot heave your heavy heart
that hurt my hollow dead.
How now like lye and bleach
the words that stunned the prose,
that purpled, that tongued –
how bleak I lunged. My love –
I thought I'd die.   How livid
I lived that vice that grip
that terrible, that ship
that rocked alone in
far-from-shore in water drought,
the short and endless parch –
that lip. How the water
the wash the words the weather
the wait healed the hurt, the heavy.

How light now my heels.
How bleached your treason.

HELP

wat sloer so in my bloed
wat byt so bokkig aan my binneboud
wat skroef wat skroei wat skreeu

wat asem
grou
peusel
teug
kreun
kwyl
suip?
wat sout?
wat duur?

Jirre help my –
ek word ding.

Ex

I refuse the word.

I resist the deletion:
the rubber of it
wants to erase
the indelible,
draw lines
through what was
good enough
for long enough.

I recant.

I reject
the language
of divorce.

It reduces
us to an error —
it makes us
a pencil slip.

MONTHS LATER, I STILL MISS THIS:

before light,
before eyes,
       a fistful of you.

before speech,
before teeth,
       unfold on to you.

before knowing,
before trying,
       break on to you.

SPELLES

Slangetjie, krulletjie he,
hoepeltjie, hoepeltjie le.

So't my ma my "school" leer spel
in haar tweede taal. Vir my was
dit die derde woord na "skool"
en "Schule".

Dis sommer net 'n storie
wat ek nooit in enige taal
vir jou vertel het nie.

Kaal lê ek teen die hitte.
Opgekrul, hangend aan 'n kussing,
slaaploos oor jou. Diep in die matras,
onder die vervelige
metronomiese masjienagtigheid
van hart en longe,
klik en tjommel
spiraalveer teen spons.

Slangetjie, krulletjie,
kom lê teen my rug;
wys my hoe
om "forget" te spel.

MEAT

I want to lick the plate where the Bratwurst lay
but I'm in the deli. I go to the cold meats counter:

a pile of thick-sliced Leberkäse, a fistful of Viennas,
rare roast beef slivered off a giant brown and pink hunk,
plate-sized slices of Gypsy Ham,
a full deck of lavender and white back bacon,
chicken breasts and thighs in an orgy of marinade,
creamy pork bangers neatly spooning beneath cling film.

Meatballs for chicken soup.
Lamb chops for later
A roast for Sunday.

I am carnivorous and out of control.
I push my flesh-laden trolley to the till,
count out bills like Monopoly money.
I am in the thrall of a vast hunger,
a terrible protein injunction.
Images of naked rumps and bellies,
of plates and palates, crowd around
the table of my mysterious need.

A baby in a pram waves his chubby legs at me.
I want to bite his thigh.

DENIAL

This is how you'll address me in the email:
> My love.
You'll say:
> My love,
> I was mistaken.
You'll say:
> I've trod the laval lip of a vast void.
You'll say:
> I reached for nacreous stars there.
You'll say:
> I tore my scars there, and, my love,
you'll say:
> I was mistaken.
> I can avoid neither love nor void,
> and perhaps the one exists because of the other.
> And will you take me, mistaken as I am, back
is what you'll ask.

You'll say:
> Will you? My love?
You'll say that.

In the email I will never receive.

You will call me your love.

My Familiar

So many months in the lost time that
my broken throat and twisted wrists
chafe familiar like someone else's shoes.

I have walked
bent wrong like this
for so long like this

yet still I ache
for the shape
of your name.

Reptilian

In the pool's clearest depths
where rocks weight silt,
I want to be scaled, gilled and slitted.
Again and again I must succumb to lungs.

Above, the boys dive off towering boulders,
the girls squeal. Ancient rituals of see me
see me fly, see me see you,
are here, below, reassuring.

Then crazy scattering:
the cobra splattering
fear into the burning day –
and nowhere for me to go but under.

The swaying reptile snakes noiseless,
essing across the surface of my ceiling.

BEACHED

My limbs are filled with sea sand packed tight
slow-moving through reluctance.
Fingers shake the coffee and cigarettes
that go in where food refuses to be held.
Inside an unhinged jaw a sea slug tongue
dithers in salt water. My eyes are wave machines.
That alone which moves is the gushing
the gushing the gushing of grief.

I am the sea shore now, patiently mindless;
weathered and constant as millennial fact.

THE QUIET WAY BACK

(With thanks to Breyten Breytenbach for his 18 perfect words embedded here)

No more words, my love, no more.
If we are to return to anything
let it be to the silence of a cathedral
larger and lighter than the thought
of a flower when a dream is the earth of a garden.
Let it be to the click and zip of things unclasped,
the creak of stairs, and footfalls towards the pews
where once we genuflected before our bodies'
better knowledge of syntax.

Peace be with you, my breast could intone,
and from deep inside, inside me, into me,
a rosary would bead back your emphatic reply:
and also with you.

ACKNOWLEDGMENTS

UCT Poetry Web and Off The Wall are the places where my private writing was transformed into its public possibilities. I thank the members of the first for their rigour and detailed, thoughtful feedback, and the members of the second for their enthusiasm.

My particular thanks goes to The Tall Men of Off The Wall – Hugh Hodge and Michael Rolfe - for whom I have both respect and great affection.

Thank you to Karen Jennings, Kandas Botha and Andries Samuel for their careful reading of my Afrikaans poems. Mistakes that remain are mine alone.

Thank you to my editor Gill Gimberg for her considered arrangement, feedback and suggestions.

And I thank Andries for his attentive input, and for negotiating the complexities of sometimes being both secret reader and first reader.

The debt I owe to those who hauled, scraped, pushed, cheered, scolded and coaxed me back from the edge is too large to be acknowledged by a miserly thank you. May your lives be blessed by an abundance of people like yourselves.

OTHER POETRY TITLES BY MODJAJI BOOKS

The Suitable Girl BY MICHELLE MCGRANE

The Everyday Wife BY PHILLIPPA YAA DE VILLIERS

missing BY BEVERLY RYCROFT

Difficult Gifts BY DAWN GARISCH

Burnt Offering BY JOAN METELERKAMP

Strange Fruit BY HELEN MOFFETT

Oleander BY FIONA ZERBST

removing BY MELISSA BUTLER

These are the Lies I Told You BY KERRY HAMMERTON

At Least the Duck Survived BY MARGARET CLOUGH

Woman Unfolding BY JENNA MERVIS

Piece Work by INGRID ANDERSEN

Please, Take Photographs BY SINDIWE MAGONA

Conduit BY SARAH FROST

Fourth Child BY MEGAN HALL

Life in Translation BY AZILA TALIT REISENBERGER